High 5

The Hand Book Of Leadership

A Five-Step Approach to
Better Leadership

Paul R. Skingle

Illustrations: New Way Solutions

ISBN: 0-97771300-8
Copyright © 2006 by Paul R. Skingle

Second English Printing: 2011
ISBN: 978-1-4583-4656-8
Copyright © 2011 by Paul R. Skingle

Spanish Version: 2011
ISBN: 978-1-4583-5929-2
Copyright © 2011 by Paul R. Skingle

All Rights Reserved
Printed in the United States

Additional copies:
For English: sales@i2isolutions.biz
For Spanish: h5-espanol@i2isolutions.biz

Contents

Books Gathering Dust

If your office bookshelf is anything like mine, it's full of "how to" books. My collection consists of management books telling me everything from the Alpha personality's tendency for an aggressive management style to leadership through the art of Zen. The only common thread among all of these wonderful and insightful manuals is that they seldom, if ever, leave the home I have made for them among the other publications from more than 30 years in leadership. Therein lies the genesis of my desire to capture key observations from time spent in large and small corporations, but with one huge difference.

This handbook is one you will always carry with you. In fact, it would be virtually impossible not to.

How? This is the handbook of your hand. Yes, *that* hand— the one on the end of your arm!

Fundamentals of Leadership

The following chapters will cover the five fundamentals of good sound leadership.

These fundamentals will see you through the majority of your daily issues with leadership, motivation, productivity, and the work environment. The premise focuses on the what and why of leadership and less on the how. Although the text is peppered with some useful hints, in my experience, there are so many variables with how things get done in an organization that debating about what does or does not work in your particular environment runs the risk of detracting from the main message. What I have found, however, is that there is almost universal agreement on what needs to get done and why companies need to address these core principles.

Where It All Started

While leading a 2,500-person mega-call center in Texas, I was asked to make a speech to the local Chamber of Commerce on leadership and the fundamentals of motivating and retaining employees.

For several days, I thought about the speech and all of the leaders with whom I had worked and observed over the years. I then started a list of the good ones and what made them stand out.

Next, I listed the leaders who were miserable to work for and what attributes made them so. After analyzing the two lists, it was interesting to see an emerging pattern. The times when I felt energized, productive and engaged with work—a true advocate for my company—there were five major items in play.

1. Clear objectives and expectations that tied into the direction of the company
2. Frequent performance feedback with helpful suggestions on ways to improve
3. Knowledgeable leaders passionate about their work
4. Acknowledgement of individuals
5. A work environment allowing employees to be at their best

On the day of the speech, I asked the audience what they would do if they were given a glossy handout. Half admitted they would throw it away while the rest would take it back to the office to file. I told them they were not going to get off that easy. They were still going to get a handout, but one they would never leave behind.

I held my left hand out and began…

For weeks afterwards, whenever I met someone at the meeting that day, the reaction was always the same. "I still remember your **hand out**," was the response. Several even went on to include that not only did the message stick, but that the 'hand out' had made it easy to take these basic principles back to the workplace. Finally, one told me, "You must get this down in writing and share it with more people." That encouragement was the inspiration for *High 5: The Hand Book of Leadership.*

The Index Finger

I started by using my index finger to point to an object across the room. Almost as one, every head in the room turned to look where I was pointing. "Why did you all look in that direction?" I asked. "Because you 'told' us to by pointing over there" was the consensus. "Good answer," I said, "and that's the first responsibility of a leader—to 'point the way' by clearly communicating the company's mission and vision."

Creating a Vision

Providing employees with direction—a vision of where the company is going—is as fundamental as leadership gets.

First and foremost is creating a vision of where you as a leader want to take the business. A vision, which can be clearly articulated, is compelling, desirable and must definitely start at the top of the organization.

Please don't confuse vision with a mission statement. We're not talking about what your organization does or hopes to do in the future. It is not about being number one in customer service, revenue or the number of widgets made, but about a passion that you have for the business.

Progress lies not in enhancing what is, but in advancing toward what will be.

KAHLIL GIBRAN

It speaks to the environment you create allowing people to reach their fullest potential. And it is up to you—the leader of the organization—to create that vision. Once you have created this future state, only then can you start building the roadmap that will take you there.

As you can see, creating the vision is the first step in the planning process that ultimately ends with everyone in the organization having a specific task linking directly back to its ultimate goal. This is the true power of the vision.

It should be possible to take any single individual in your organization and define a clear path from day-to-day tasks to how that person's job fits in with the vision and mission of the organization. And I mean **EVERY** job. In fact, it is fair to say that if you cannot make this linkage, then it should raise a red flag as to the validity of that particular job function.

The following matrix aligns the company around specific goals and harnesses the synergies of the entire organization.

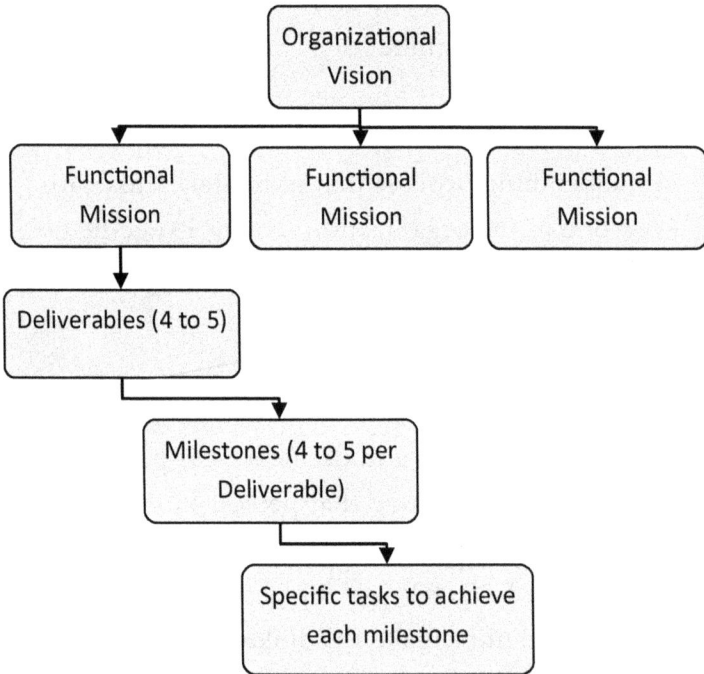

```
                    ┌─────────────────┐
                    │ Organizational  │
                    │     Vision      │
                    └─────────────────┘
         ┌───────────────────┼───────────────────┐
┌─────────────┐     ┌─────────────┐     ┌─────────────┐
│ Functional  │     │ Functional  │     │ Functional  │
│  Mission    │     │  Mission    │     │  Mission    │
└─────────────┘     └─────────────┘     └─────────────┘
       │
┌─────────────────────┐
│ Deliverables (4 to 5)│
└─────────────────────┘
          │
     ┌──────────────────────┐
     │ Milestones (4 to 5 per│
     │    Deliverable)       │
     └──────────────────────┘
               │
          ┌──────────────────────┐
          │ Specific tasks to achieve│
          │    each milestone       │
          └──────────────────────┘
```

Organizational or company vision statements are not as easy as they appear and are often very personal and emotional.

The 60-second Commercial

Using 60 seconds for each step, can you accomplish the following?

Your Company Vision

What future state is your company trying to achieve that is desirable for your employees, customers and shareholders?

Your Departmental Vision

What is the mission of your department that helps support the company vision?

Your Employees' Task

How does the work your employee performs tie into the departmental mission and company vision?

For example, if you were a world-class figure skater, saying that you want to be the number one figure skater in the world is a mission—NOT a vision. The vision would go something like this: Close your eyes and imagine that you are standing on top of the winner's podium in an arena with the crowd shouting, "USA! USA!" The spotlight bathes you in a warm glow as you bend your head to receive the gold medal. As you stand, your body feels lighter than air. Your vision has become a reality.

This *vision* can drive a skater to new heights of performance. What comes afterward is everything the skater needs to do to make this vision come true.

The *mission* of becoming the number one skater in the world will drive deliverables, such as obtaining rink practice times, getting a coach and planning competition schedules. But it all starts with the vision.

There's one other step to keep in mind. And again, it relates to giving clear and unambiguous direction. It's the **SMART** goal.

Establishing SMART Goals

On the surface, setting goals always seems to be a simple exercise. Yet it has been the undoing of some very good leaders. Many missteps result from a fundamental lack of communication, which can be easily remedied by following a few simple basic rules. In fact, these rules even come with their own handy acronym—**SMART** goals.

S = Specific

Perhaps the beginning of most misunderstandings is not being specific about what the goal actually is. A goal such as, "You need to have better results next month," seems absurd when you read it. But how many times have you heard managers provide this type of direction and then justify it by saying, "Well, he knows what I mean. He knows what the goals are." In this age of flattened organizations and focus on increased productivity, a majority of the workforce has more than one responsibility.

Be specific. If it is increased sales, then say so. If it is reduced attrition, then say it clearly and make sure your goals are not in conflict. For instance, a single goal to reduce overtime in the distribution department can result in late shipments. In turn this sends conflicting messages and potentially results in a seesaw, "flavor of the month" type of operation.

M = Measurable

Remember the old axiom, "Measurement is management's way of saying they care"? Use of words, such as *better, more of, or less of,* should be banned from any goal setting. What does *better* mean? Is it meeting all of the goals? Is it being 25 percent better than this month? How about when an employee comes back smiling next month because of a 10 percent improvement from last month? This is NOT the time to say, "Well, that's not good enough. I wanted a 40 percent improvement."

A = Attainable

If your goal is to demoralize your workforce, then start by setting unattainable goals. Remember that people work best when they are achieving, not when continuing to fail. There is no harm, however, in setting goals that have several levels, often called 'stretch goals'. Just make sure that a stretch goal has the possibility to be achieved. If people feel defeated before they even start, then you have achieved nothing. In fact, you will have done far more harm than good.

R = Relevant

There are two schools of thought around the "r". Some like to use *realistic,* but I think if your goals are specific, measurable and attainable, they are very likely to be realistic. I prefer *relevant.* Relevant means: Can you tie the goal back to a milestone or deliverable of the functional organization? If not, then rethink why you are setting the goal in the first place.

T = Time Bound

Goals should be given a beginning and an end to ensure that they get done. By establishing time checks along the life span of a goal, you are demonstrating that the goal has meaning and relevance to you and the organization. In addition, it has established your own accountability to the process and enables you to offer advice and encouragement.

When you look at your index finger, think of pointing the organization in the right direction and providing clear and unambiguous goals to those who look to you for leadership.

Our plans miscarry because they have no aim. When a man does not know what harbor he is making for, no wind is the right wind.

SENECA

The Thumb

With my thumb pointing up, I asked the audience to describe what it saw, and more importantly, what this hand position meant. There was no doubt in their minds. "Positive feedback," someone called out. "Job well done," said another. I pointed my thumb down and asked, "Now what do you see? The unanimous sentiment, "Bad news."

Power of Feedback

In Roman times, the thumb was used to provide the ultimate in feedback. Thumbs-up meant life and positive recognition for the gladiator. Thumbs-down signaled pretty much the end of things—figuratively and literally!

Hopefully, we have made progress since then toward a more civilized path. However, if you have run up against The Intimidator boss, who believes that nothing can be achieved without his or her verbal abuse preceding any directive and retribution following any action, you might well question just how far we have really progressed.

Feedback remains the most powerful gift one individual can give to another and it carries with it the burden of using it wisely. I have seen it used to great effect to elevate performance. And I also have seen it used to destroy.

Coach vs. Referee

I don't normally use sports metaphors, but this one has particular meaning for leadership. Ask yourself this question: Do people see me more as a coach or a referee?

In most sports, the role of a referee is to catch the players doing something wrong. The player's role then becomes one of getting away with as much as possible by pushing or bending the rules until the whistle is blown.

Contrast this with the coach. To help each player reach full potential, a coach strives for optimum performance. A good leader will see how each individual can contribute fully to the team and will hold each player accountable for his or her actions and contributions.

As leaders, we give feedback for two basic reasons:

⇒ To encourage positive performance

⇒ To correct poor performance or to bring an end to undesirable behaviors

Encourage Positive Performance

Feedback comes in two basic forms. The first is when we are coaching for optimal performance. The role of leader as a coach is significant in the development of the people who look to us for leadership. It is during this type of coaching when an employee is most likely to reach peak performance.

By following this three-step process, you will set yourself up to be a successful coach:

1) Identify the reason for the coaching session.

- An individual has new needs or desires new skills.
- There are new challenges that require a different set of competencies for individuals or the entire team.
- The direction of the organization is changing and there will be new future needs.

2) Define the scope of the coaching.

- Responsibility: Will the team or an individual be expected to accomplish a new skill or process? Being vague will not be helpful. You must be as specific as possible. Remember you can always modify along the way.

- Authority: Clearly identify the available resources during the scope of this coaching initiative. This might range from formal classes and budgetary amounts to the use of company time and access to mentors.
- Accountability: How will the success of the coaching be measured? What milestones will there be along the way?

3) Initiate the feedback cycle.

- Feedback will be more frequent in the beginning and reduced as the comfort level grows. Depending on the length of the coaching effort, this could be daily at first and then move to weekly.
- Feedback is important and should be a non-negotiable calendar item for all involved.
- As coach, your role is to remove obstacles, obtain resources and provide encouragement.

Correct Poor Performance or Bring an End to Undesirable Behaviors

In this role, providing feedback becomes less the function of a coach and more like that of a referee. First determine if you are dealing with the early stages of a performance issue or a chronic problem involving either performance or a violation of policy and procedures.

For performance issues, follow the three-step process for successful coaching but with one additional step— consequences! This fourth step is crucial and must clearly state what the consequences are if the performance issue is not corrected.

Violations of policy and procedures or chronic performance failures are things that must be addressed quickly and effectively. Regardless of your leadership position, your credibility will be on the line if you do not deal with chronic issues in a timely manner. Seek guidance from your manager and human resource professional.

But is all feedback created equal? The answer is no. Whether or not it is positive feedback or constructive criticism, for feedback to be meaningful, it should fit the *RIMS* profile. While the *SMART* goals use the basic rules for goal setting, the *RIMS* profile provides a step-by-step guideline for giving effective feedback.

RIMS Profile

- Relevant
- Immediate
- Meaningful and Measurable
- Sincere and Specific

Relevant

Relevant means your feedback should be related to the action or event currently being observed and/or specifically anchored to a place or time. It is confusing to the recipient (and makes you look disorganized) if the feedback is about an action completely unrelated to what the person is currently doing.

Immediate

Feedback is most effective when it is given as close to the action as possible. The longer you wait, the less impact the feedback will have. In fact, if well-deserved positive feedback is delayed long enough it can be demoralizing. On the other hand, if the intent of feedback was to correct negative behavior, not speaking up sooner could have unwittingly condoned the wrong behavior.

Meaningful and Measurable

Feedback should be meaningful and appropriate to the situation. For example, saying, "Nice job," to someone who worked all weekend on a project saving the company millions of dollars is not very meaningful. By the same token, someone who came in an hour early to help finish a report doesn't need to receive a bouquet of roses or be recognized in the company newsletter.

Giving feedback against some measurable goal is very powerful and can be instrumental in people striving harder to reach that next level.

Sincere and Specific

Have you ever interacted with an individual whose feedback was completely self-serving and insincere? Phony feedback can be worse than none at all.

Great job, whoever

you are, whatever

you did.

In an internal consulting role, I once coached a manager who was rated low on giving feedback. Apparently, after attending a training session on management skills, he scheduled in his day planner to go out at 4:00 p.m. every day to give feedback to his team. Although his intentions were well meaning, he came across as forced and phony. He was perceived as simply checking off another item from a to-do list, rather than sincerely thinking about what he said.

Giving specific and detailed feedback will leave the recipient with no doubts about your intentions. In fact, it demonstrates that you actually took time and cared enough about what you said.

Case Study

As the manager of a call center, you have just completed a side-by-side monitoring session with John. He handled a particularly tricky customer situation very well, however, there were additional resources overlooked that may have helped him. You debrief the call immediately.

> **Relevant Feedback:** "John, I liked the way you handled the customer's concern with our product. You acknowledged his feelings without being defensive and asked open-ended questions to help understand the specifics of his concern."
>
> **Non-relevant Feedback:** "John, that call was good, but I want to talk to you about being late yesterday."

Immediate

In our case study, the manager met with John immediately after the call-coaching session. This reinforced positive behaviors. If the manager were unable to meet with John right away, then a valid alternative would be to set a specific time and place to review the calls.

Meaningful

Based on our case study, here is a hierarchy of feedback levels that help illustrate this point:

1. Good job.
2. Good job, John.
3. Good job on this series of calls, John.
4. Good job on this series of calls, John. I particularly liked the way you used open-ended questions to probe for more detail.
5. Good job on this series of calls, John. I particularly liked the way you used open-ended questions to probe for more detail. It makes me feel really good that you're part of the team.

As you can see, always operating at level five runs the risk of diluting the effectiveness of any feedback. By varying the level, you will find people responding accordingly.

Specific

Be specific—especially when the feedback is not all positive. It is important to be as inclusive as possible and start out on a positive note. In our case study, John missed a resource that may have helped him. The feedback session could go something like this:

> *"John, on call number two with Mr. Brown, I liked the way you handled the customer's concern with our product. You acknowledged his feelings without being defensive and asked open-ended questions to help understand the specifics of his concern. You used Mr. Brown's name three times and always asked his permission when putting him on hold. You also serviced the call every 30 seconds to relieve any anxiety he might have felt. If a similar situation arises, I recommend that you reference section six of the product manual. It will help you resolve these types of concerns."*

Sincere

An excellent way to demonstrate sincerity is to engage in a dialogue with the person receiving the feedback. Our case study example might go something like this:

"John, now that I have given my observations regarding your calls, I'd like to hear how you felt about them. Tell me what you believe you did particularly well and perhaps what you might do differently next time?"

When you look at your thumb, think about how you can become the greatest coach in the world—and not just a referee. When the people you are leading receive well thought-out feedback, they will be on the way to peak performance.

The Ring Finger

The next logical finger was my middle one. An audible gasp—and some chuckling—erupted as I carefully examined this digit of universal expression. "Well," I said, "I'm not going there right now, but trust me, we will come back to it!" Then I held up my ring finger showing my wedding band, which hasn't come off in more than 30 years. "What does this mean to you?" I asked. "Commitment," said one. "Passion," said another. Precisely," I said.

Ancient Egyptian writings assert that a very delicate nerve runs from the fourth finger of the left hand to the heart, thus accounting for its current use as the wedding-ring finger in Western cultures. A ring is a perfect circle; a symbol of unity and passion that every leader strives to achieve as a goal for his or her team.

So here is the big question you should ask yourself: If I am not totally engaged in the business and showing my own passion and enthusiasm on a daily basis, how can I expect my team to be any different?

Welcome to management and leadership. You have just given up the right to have a bad day. Whatever happened at home this morning or however bad yesterday was, your team deserves nothing less than your best every time you interact with them. Give what you expect in return. Nothing short of being a passionate and committed role model is good enough for the ring finger.

Alignment and Empowerment

Alignment - Commitment to the goals and directions of an organization.

Empowerment - The ability to act without waiting to be told what to do.

While the index finger provides the organization with direction and establishes goals and objectives (alignment), it is the ring finger that symbolizes empowerment. It is through empowerment that people show passion for their company. They take actions that can inspire peak performance. In fact, the interaction of these two powerful forces produces some interesting results.

The Victim

With low alignment and empowerment, The Victim is not committed to the direction of the company and feels totally powerless to change his situation.

The Loose Cannon

With high empowerment but low alignment, The Loose Cannon seeks a high degree of personal involvement and action but tends to create havoc and uncertainty.

The Guard

In this instance, high alignment has The Guard fiercely protecting his turf and more concerned with doing things right than doing the right thing. Low empowerment makes The Guard unable to inspire employees and to reach out across departmental boundaries.

The Enlightened Leader

With high alignment and empowerment, The Enlightened Leader provides clear direction and inspires employees to action!

50

We are all faced with a series of great opportunities brilliantly disguised as unsolvable problems.

JOHN W. GARDNER

Personal Empowerment

Empowerment of your team rests with you and starts with your own empowerment. Personal empowerment requires three key elements:

♦   Problem solver
♦   Industry expert
♦   Source of knowledge

Problem Solver

Being an effective problem solver is less about having one or two specific skills than your attitude toward problems and your ability to anticipate them. There are as many ways to solve problems as there are problems to be solved.

I have always liked the story that author Joel Barker recalls in his book, *Discovering the Future*, about a young man who just loved to ride in his new sports-car convertible. On one particularly fine day, he found himself alone on a country road that was barely wide enough for one car with no one else in sight. The sun was sparkling through the trees, and he had not a care in the world.

With enthusiasm, he floored the accelerator and roared down the country lane. Fast approaching a bend in the road, he was horrified to see a woman rounding the corner—on the wrong side of the road!

The collision was imminent when, at the very last minute, the woman swerved over to her side of the road. She called out to the young man narrowly missing his prize possession, "Pig!" "How dare she," he thought, "I was right and she was wrong." "Sow!" he yells back over his shoulder. Feeling smug at having gotten in the last word, he once again floored the accelerator, shot around the corner...........

……….and ran right into a pig!

When a problem comes careening around a corner, do you view it as an opportunity or as an inevitable catastrophe that has been sent to derail your brilliant career?

Leaders who view problems as opportunities will:

♦ Build contingency plans
♦ Consider multiple outcomes and scenarios
♦ Have alternate options available
♦ Use problems to challenge the status quo and encourage new ideas

Industry Expert

Become an industry expert by subscribing to industry magazines and periodicals. Find out if there are any associations in your industry (few industries are without some type of association) and join a local chapter. Search the Internet, join news groups and subscribe to e-mail lists for newsletters. A colleague once told me that if you were to read literature on a single topic for two hours per day, within a year you would be considered one of the world's leading experts on that topic! Just think of the knowledge you could gain if you were to read an article or do research on your industry for 30 minutes every workday. In a very short time people would turn to you as an expert source of information.

Source of Knowledge

In a recent survey, employees were asked to name the person they looked to for information about the company and industry in which they worked. More than 70 percent answered their immediate supervisor. Your credibility is on the line.

If asked, could you recite the factors that determine your department's success and where you stand vis-à-vis your goals? Do you know and understand your company's vision statement? Can you articulate your department's mission statement? If the answer to these questions is yes, then congratulations. Your employees see you as a source of knowledge about the business and the company. If not, then get busy and find the answers. There are many ways to increase your knowledge about the company. For example, check with your boss. Read the annual report. Ask permission to attend other department staff meetings. Or, invite your boss' manager to join one of your own team meetings.

Empowering Employees

Empowering employees comes from many different sources including establishing trust, not "shooting the messenger", sharing information, setting appropriate goals (see the Index Finger) and providing open, honest and timely feedback (see the Thumb).

But one particularly successful way is to practice effective delegation. So often, delegation can look a lot like "dumping" to an employee. By following these three steps, you can avoid this common pitfall.

Effective Delegation

Responsibility

What is it specifically that you want the person to do? Spell it out in as much detail as possible. NEVER assume something is obvious and does not need direction. I recommend this be done in writing. But if that is not possible, ask the person to repeat back to you his or her understanding of the task.

Authority

Detail what the limits are for this project in terms of manpower, budget, spending authorization, travel or any other resources that may be necessary.

Accountability

Be specific about how you are going to measure their success. What will a successful outcome look like?

Many new employees making their way up the corporate ladder love to be given increased responsibility as a form of recognition and additional authority as an outward sign of that recognition. Oftentimes, employees resist the idea of additional accountability. But without accountability there can be no recognition, and without recognition there can be no reward.

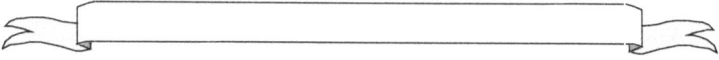

Teachable Moments

Another key element to personal empowerment is to look for "teachable
moments," both for you and others. You
probably have many teachable moments
tucked away but do not necessarily think
of them in those terms. One particularly
effective way is to assign each member of
your team a specific topic that can be
taught within 30 minutes and shared with
the group. It is important for you to
participate as well. Make sure the topics
are relevant to the business and provide
support and guidance. This demonstrates
a willingness to continually learn (a key
behavior of successful leaders) and a
desire to grow the potential of your
employees.

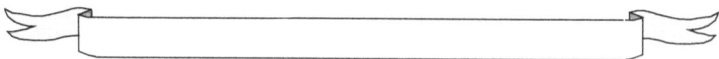

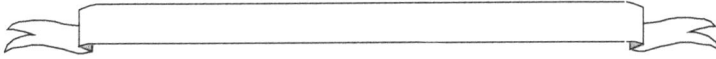

For example, one of my managers was having a service problem with help-desk turnaround time. He was obviously frustrated at not being able to resolve the issue, so I helped him map out the processes of how his help desk resolved customer issues. Quite honestly, I hadn't considered my knowledge of process mapping as anything out of the ordinary. For this supervisor, however, it was like seeing his business in an entirely different light. Based on this new insight, he restructured his help desk and solved the turnaround time to not only meet but exceed his customers' expectations. As a leader, it was a very gratifying moment and encouraged me to look for similar ways to help my staff in the future.

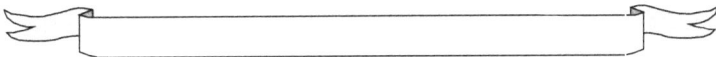

When you look at your ring finger, think of all the great accomplishments in our global society. Two things always seem to shine through—passion and commitment. Sometimes it resonates in the commitment of quiet determination and in others a fiery passion that ignites the world.

The Little Finger

"Have you ever heard the expression, 'A stitch in time saves nine' or 'Look after the pennies and the pounds will look after themselves'?" I asked. They are admonishing us to look after the little things in life. Things that, if ignored, can become a disaster for us both personally and professionally. I raised my small pinky finger and told the audience, "I call this the 'interpersonal' finger; the one that draws our attention to the personal side of life. Ignore this at your peril!"

Appreciation

For many, the absence of even the smallest amount of appreciation can be devastating. This e-mail was recently sent to the CEO of a large international firm.

> *"The reason I write you this e-mail is to voice my sadness and also to share my opinion with you. I have been working for this company for more than eight years as an executive assistant at one of the branches and I resigned at the beginning of this year.*

> *"Over the past eight years, I have worked so hard for [the company] but I noticed that the management did not show any appreciation for administrators like me—not only in [the] U.S. but all of the locations around the world."*

The effect of attrition on a company's bottom line can be large indeed. The cost of replacing this executive assistant will run into thousands of dollars in recruiting, training and lost productivity, not to mention the loss of loyalty. So this is not just about "being nice." It is about a direct impact to your company by not paying attention to something that costs absolutely nothing!

This example also tells us that there are two aspects to the little finger: What do people want and what are you capable of giving?

What People Want

Frederick Herzberg is considered the father of job enrichment and one of the major management philosophers of our time. I studied his work while researching a course I was facilitating on motivation and leadership and was fascinated by the simplicity of his findings and the far-reaching impact they had on the workplace.

Factors that strongly determined job satisfaction:
- Achievement
- Recognition
- Work itself
- Responsibility
- Advancement

Factors that strongly determined job dissatisfaction:
- Company policy
- Administration policies
- Supervision
- Salary
- Interpersonal relations
- Working conditions

The rule of the little finger is simple when it comes to others. You, the leader, are responsible for creating the environment in which others can succeed. You must set the example. You can see why the individual in the e-mail decided to leave the company. She was clearly not receiving recognition for her contribution to the success of the organization or any acknowledgement that she even existed. All of this could have been avoided by positive attention from her manager.

The things people say positively impact their job experiences are not the opposite of what they say negatively impact their experience.

FREDERICK HERZBERG

It is interesting to note that the last three "satisfiers"—work itself, responsibility, and advancement—were also the most important for bringing about lasting changes in employee attitudes. If you want an engaged workforce, employees must have work that they find meaningful with a commensurate level of responsibility and the opportunity, should they wish it, for advancement.

There are some big questions you need to ask yourself about how people are treated in your organization. Is there acknowledgement? Appreciation? Respect? Check off the factors that provide job satisfaction and see where you stack up. Better yet, ask your employees to do it as well.

Have you ever had a boss who treated you simply as a number? A work environment that showed zero interest in you as a person and left you feeling dissatisfied? Well, ranking right up there with salary as a job dissatisfier is interpersonal skills—or perhaps we should say lack of them.

Case for Interpersonal Skills

A study of "executive derailers," conducted at the Center for Effective Leadership, highlighted four of the key elements most likely to sink an executive career.

Failure to deliver on promises

o   Over-committing and under-delivering

o   Failure to follow through

o   Betrayal of trust

Poor interpersonal skills

o   Arrogant and intimidating

o   Insensitive to others

o   Manipulative

o   Overly critical

Not adaptable to change

o   Inability to alter behavior

o   Inflexible

Failure to build and lead an effective team

o   Micromanagement

o   Refusal to delegate

o   Isolated

Of the four, the most often cited was poor interpersonal skills. You would think an executive would recognize this need and try to do something about it. A common problem is that leaders have been rewarded for getting results regardless of the cost and, as a consequence, have sacrificed employees on the altar of profitability.

Make no mistake—many executives DO recognize that they have interpersonal issues. The problem is they often choose to do nothing about it. Instead, they huddle in self-affirming groups and talk about how:

- **They're not here to be liked.**
- **They need "edge" to be successful in business.**
- **If you're being nice, you're not getting the most out of people.**
- **Workers need to fear them in order to produce maximum results.**

What many fail to see is that the very aggressiveness of their outward behaviors creates the situations they are trying desperately to avoid.

The Truth Hurts

A group of highly tenured employees worked in a department responsible for setting customer service policies and procedures for a major corporation. One aspect of their job description was answering customer correspondence addressed to the departmental vice president.

The vice president was a classic autocratic manager who led by yelling and screaming, and made it quite clear he would never be satisfied with first or second drafts of any letter regardless of its merits.

This became so demoralizing that the employees devised a plan. They retrieved a letter from the archives personally written by the vice president. They then inserted an appropriate paragraph into a new customer letter and sent it along for his approval. It gave the employees no small amount of pleasure when the letter was returned with a glaring red line through the paragraph the vice president had previously authored, with a margin note that literally said, "What idiot wrote this piece of s@#*?" The response, "You did," was followed shortly by a departmental meeting.

73

Objectivity is the Key

Being an effective interpersonal leader starts with a willingness to take an objective look at your own leadership personality. Few people are born great leaders. Most are perfected through diligent and sincere hard work. They improve through behavior-focused self-development, while optimizing their strengths and focusing on areas for improvement.

A good three-step process for highly effective self-development includes:

- **Knowing yourself**
- **Understanding how others see you**
- **Creating a development plan**

Know Yourself

This is not as obvious as it sounds. I have met many
people who have no idea why they act and react in
certain ways. We tend to clearly see those things that fit
with our view of the world. They make sense to us and
we readily accept them as the truth. In fact, it is often
difficult for us to fathom why other people don't see
things as clearly as we do. So it comes as a complete
shock when other people see our leadership
differently. What you believe are your strengths, others
might see as a weakness.

For example, you might pride yourself on honesty, while
many others see you as insensitive. You pay attention to
detail and others see you as micro-managing. You are a
perfectionist, but others see you as nit-picky. The list is
endless and the end results are never productive.

The first step to gaining greater understanding of yourself
is by trying to find out why you react the way you do.
What hardwiring exists within to make you unique? One
way to do this is by completing a personality inventory.
There are many excellent instruments available today. The
best known and the one I have used most often is the
Myers-Briggs Type Indicator (MBTI®).

Understand How Others See You

Large Organizations

Most large organizations will have some form of 360°
feedback used for gathering information on leadership
effectiveness. Use it! Often, we have blind spots to our
own leadership persona. A targeted 360° feedback report
focusing on desired
behaviors will ensure
that you are
developing your
strengths as well as
correcting the
weaknesses keeping
you from being an
extraordinary leader.

Small Organizations

Even if the size of the organization doesn't lend itself to
360° feedback, you can still determine how others see you
by participating in a manager or executive assimilation
process. An assimilation process is basically a confidential
assessment of an individual leader's strengths and
weaknesses conducted by an impartial facilitator.

Create a Development Plan

Write it down, share it and give it life! As the saying goes, the road to hell is paved with good intentions. Most personal development plans fail because they don't meet the **SMART** criteria. In personal development plans, we add one more "s" and make it the **SMARTS** criteria. The final "s" stands for **share**. Share your development plan with your manager, and as appropriate, your team. Enlisting the help of others and expressing your own accountability to change is an important motivating factor.

People want to know that you, their leader, care about them. Your challenge is to tailor your approach to meet those individual needs. The simplest way is to get to know your employees as individuals. Ask people about their family, their career ambitions, and what they do outside of work. Maintain an open-door policy, be approachable and, above all, pay attention to the little things.

79

The Middle Finger

At this point, there was an audible gasp from the audience. They wondered, "Is he really going to hold up THAT finger?" "I know what you're thinking," I said. "And yes, I am, because this finger is the most misunderstood. You absolutely cannot afford to 'piss-off' your employees. I have seen more people leave organizations—not because they couldn't perform, but because a hostile work environment drove them away."

Productivity and motivation will never spring spontaneously from a hostile work environment!

Most people believe a workplace is hostile only if there is some form of harassment taking place. There is no doubt that harassment in a workplace is absolutely hostile. But so is the promise of training that is never delivered, benefits not materialized and a pension plan conveniently defaulted in bankruptcy. Get the picture?

As a leader, the impact of the environment you create cannot be understated. Recently, I was talking with a colleague about the various reasons why employees leave a company. After all, a job change can be very unsettling and a substantial barrier to leaving a current employer. So what are the main reasons someone does it? According to my attrition-savvy friend, employees leave for two main reasons:

♦ Feelings of inadequacy
♦ It is easier than trying to change the system.

Feelings of Inadequacy

Did you ever feel out of your depth with no place to turn? At best, it made you feel uncomfortable. Or worse, you felt incompetent or even stupid. Inadequacy comes from many different factors and often can be ingrained soon after employment.

84

It usually starts when new-hires are doomed to failure through insufficient training, tools or processes. In most situations, new employees have a window of opportunity in which to feel competent. Depending upon the job, this window usually closes after approximately 45 days. At this crucial time, you will see the highest attrition rate.

However, the feeling of inadequacy is not unique to new employees. How often have you witnessed this scenario? A good supervisor leading a team gets promoted to a manager's position and is now in charge of several teams. In this totally different ballgame, the newly promoted manager struggles with the expanded responsibilities.

Senior management, with an all too common "sink or swim" attitude, has unwittingly created a hostile environment for this new manager. Soon, feelings of inadequacy set in and the manager faces a lose-lose option—quit or fail!

Leaving is Easier Than Trying to Change the System

The second reason runs a little deeper for many employees. They tire of being treated as a liability and feel it is easier to leave than to stay and argue. For example, a company located in a rural part of the country had a large single-parent population as its primary source of recruitment. Instead of designing systems and policies to accommodate this rich source of labor, the company completely disregarded how this demographic would impact the business. Rather than initiating creative ideas—such as flextime or job-sharing—to accommodate this particular workforce, the company was inflexible because of rules that could not (or would not) be broken. The results were inevitable. Within a year, the personnel turnover was more than 120 percent. Within three years, the company had gone through the area's entire eligible population! Frantic measures were taken to recruit, but by then it was too late. Nobody wanted to work for a company with such inflexible policies designed to fire rather than to work with employees. Any kind of change is extremely difficult, but in a hostile work environment employees would rather leave than try and change a system that does not meet their basic needs.

Create the Right Environment

For a majority of employees, the most important relationship is the one with their immediate supervisor. So the primary responsibility of every supervisor should be cultivating this interaction. It is frustrating to find that this is barely given lip service in most organizations. Instead, the current trend is toward increased spans of control, with supervisors becoming little more than policemen tasked with catching people in the act of wrongdoing. In addition, they're burdened with more and more administrative work.

It is ironic that in most industries—both services and manufacturing—the success of the enterprise has been placed in the hands of the lowest seniority and least-trained members of the organization. Consequently, the support that supervisors give to frontline employees becomes nothing short of survival.

Think how differently workers would be treated if viewed as highly paid surgeons. Work areas would be carefully planned for optimum efficiency and a surgeon would never be asked to stop in the middle of an operation and search for a tool or part that wasn't readily available.

Moving from autocratic to performance-based management is never easy. For years management has been rewarded for meeting the numbers, regardless of how many laid-off employees are left behind.

There is hope for the future. With commitment from the top, I have witnessed large corporations making concerted efforts to change their culture. Most started with an open and sincere analysis of the current state within the organization. A detailed vision of the future became the basis for clearly expressed measures of success, and the result was a roadmap to a compelling and desirable future.

Keep in mind that such a roadmap is not just an intellectual exercise. It is about gaining a *competitive advantage* in your marketplace. When processes, infrastructure and locations can be replicated within weeks—if not days or hours—the one true advantage for any business is its people.

HOTEL HACIENDA
COCOYOC

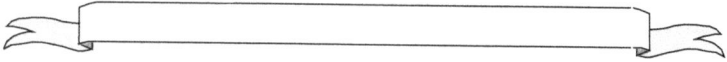

An Ideal Working Environment in an Idyllic Setting

If you do not think your employees are your most effective and valuable asset, just look to the wonderful resort of Hacienda Cocoyoc, owned and operated by the Rivera Torres family under the direction of Paulino Rivera Torres Mansi.

The History: Cocoyoc is unique in many ways. Its long history goes as far back as the Nahuatl and Aztec Indian empires. Part of the territory was given to Herman Cortes after the Conquest of Mexico in 1521. However, the history of the actual hotel begins in the 1600s as crop land for

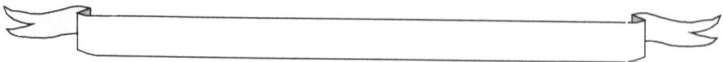

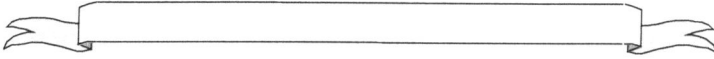

the peasants. During this period, the Hacienda received a government license to set up a horse-driven sugar mill for processing sugar cane. By the end of the century, Hacienda Cocoyoc consisted of 366 acres of irrigated land, a house, chapel, sugar mill and other plantation buildings. Its importance grew at the beginning of the nineteenth century with the construction of beautifully arched stone aqueducts for irrigation, many of which are still in service today.

Until 1910, the Hacienda continued to flourish. At that time, Emiliano Zapata, an agrarian revolutionary, and his followers burned and destroyed many haciendas, including the Hacienda Cocoyoc, as symbols of peasant oppression. In 1957, Paulino Rivera Torres (the father of the current owners) saw the potential of the Hacienda Cocoyoc and carried out his

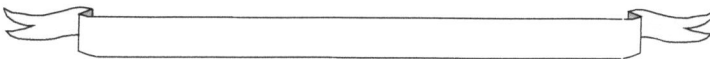

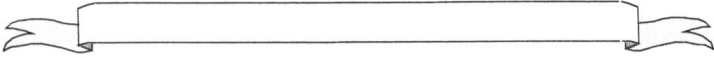

dream of turning the Hacienda into a self-functioning first-class resort.

The Mission: The overriding sense at Hacienda Cocoyoc is one of pride and values for all people who work at the resort, regardless of the position they hold. The resort is very process-driven; however, the processes control the operation, not the people. In fact, Paulino and his staff describe the Hacienda Cocoyoc mission in an intriguing way.

"There is a feeling of identity, motivated by an ambience of fairness, trust and freedom, among the people who work at Hacienda Cocoyoc. They understand the common good and teamwork as the most important parts of their commitment to all of the hotel shareholders and their objectives. Flexibility in all types of work generates a sense of equality, support and solidarity that allows service to flow in a more natural way. Supervision is rare; it is mostly process control and the

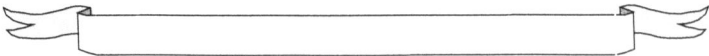

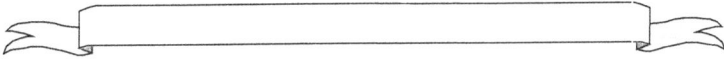

improvement of the system that prevail as a common goal in the leadership at Hacienda Cocoyoc. The time devoted to workshops is oriented mainly to the development of people, character and a positive attitude, rather than just to information, as the ability to do their work is achieved through loyalty, practice and a commitment to the mission of the resort as a whole."

Guiding Hand: With such collaborative and nurturing guidance, the Hacienda Cocoyoc environment embodies all five principles of leadership. From giving clear direction, feedback, commitment, and attention to detail, Paulino and his "extended Cocoyoc family" have created the ultimate vision of a positive working environment that not only nurtures its employees, but is a highly successful working model. This model is truly an inspiration on every level.

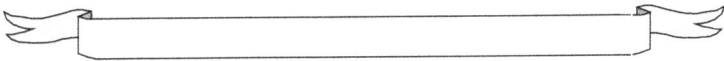

When I look at my middle finger, I am reminded that one of the most critical responsibilities we have as leaders is to create an environment in which others can excel. I was always humbled by the thought that if I missed one day of work the business continued as usual. But if one of my employees failed to show up, the company lost money. It definitely pays to create a hostile-free work environment.

The Hand

Once again I held out my entire hand. "There you have it," I said. "A handout you will never leave behind with all of the answers right there—at the end of your fingertips! Now that you have the complete hand in front of you, think about how it ties together. It is, by design, a simple building block."

Starting with the index finger, you should think of how well your employees are aligned. Do they understand where you are trying to take the business? Have they bought in to the process? Do they understand WIIFM (What's In It For Me) so that you are not setting up a scenario where they check their brains at the door when they come to work? Are your directions clear and your goals **SMART**?

How do your employees receive feedback? Is it formal, informal or a combination of both? Can progress and success be self-monitored? I've seen organizations where feedback was like bowling but with a curtain halfway down the lane. The employee throws the ball, which goes under the curtain and he or she is rewarded with the sound of toppling pins. The supervisor stands at the curtain and says, "You hit six pins," but doesn't say which pins fell or where to aim the next ball. Imagine the frustration of being given only half the picture. An educated employee is a tremendous asset, and making sure feedback is accessible and meaningful will pay incredible dividends.

A chicken and a pig walked past a restaurant advertising a breakfast special of bacon and eggs. The chicken looked at the sign and said to the pig, "I'm contributing to that special." "Indeed you are," said the pig, "but I'm committed to it!" Leadership is more than just giving orders, it's about commitment to the business AND your people!

Always try to remember a few golden rules regarding the little finger:

+ Get out of the office and go to where the work gets done.
+ Smile and be approachable.
+ Maintain the self-confidence and self-esteem of the people with whom you interact.
+ Listen, listen and listen! You never learn anything new when you are doing all of the talking.
+ Ask questions and show genuine interest.
+ Take the initiative to leave things better than how you found them.
+ Always remember to follow through on promises made.

The key driver of the little finger is acknowledgement. There are so many related feelings wrapped around this concept. By asking people what recognition means to them, you get an appreciation of the little finger's enormous impact. Ask how someone felt after receiving acknowledgement and you will hear sentiments such as, "I felt appreciated, respected, trusted and motivated."

Often asked about my leadership style, my answer is always the same: I strive to create an environment in which others can excel. Webster's dictionary defines a leader as a guide or conductor—someone who provides direction. In the majority of cases the leader doesn't actually do the physical task, just as a music conductor doesn't play an instrument in the orchestra. A true leader is responsible for creating the music by leading the musicians. Often you hear that the great conductors of the world are celebrated for their ability to derive music from an orchestra and surpass the audience expectations.

How do they do this? By creating an environment in which every single musician, instrument and nuance of the music achieves its pinnacle of performance. This would be impossible if the environment fostered angry individuals rather than a cohesive unit.

My favorite definition of leadership comes from a workshop participant who said, "Leadership is letting other people have your way." That is it—put very succinctly indeed!

Each finger—in and of itself—is only one part of a whole. Realize that the business world requires your entire hand to make it work. Use this tool as a guiding hand so that others will seek to join and support you and the organization.

Now Give Yourself a Hand!

Thumbs-up

To my great friend and colleague, Jorge Gaitan. Without your long-term vision and determined mission, the Spanish version would never have been possible. Muchas gracias, mi amigo.

To the wonderful Hacienda Cocoyoc 'family' for your commitment and detail to the "little things" of life. And most of all, to our gracious host, Paulino, for your wonderful hospitality.

To my fabulous family and friends—you know who you are and make the fabric of my life a wonderful environment and a beautiful place to be.

And to Aimee—with you everything is possible.